Self Esteem

The Self Help Book for Women and Men eager to Improve Self Confidence and Overcome Self Doubt

Regina Williams

Table of Contents

SELF ESTEEM	**1**
INTRODUCTION	**5**
CHAPTER 1	**7**
WHAT IS LOW SELF-ESTEEM	7
How to Develop Self-Confidence	*13*
CHAPTER 2	**18**
WHY IS SELF-ESTEEM IMPORTANT?	18
SIZES OF SELF-ESTEEM	20
CHAPTER 3	**24**
GREAT THINGS ABOUT HIGH SELF-ESTEEM	24
What's Self-Esteem and Why could it be Important?	*25*
10 Most Common Great Things About Having High Self-Esteem	*27*
CHAPTER 4	**33**
IMPORTANCE OF HIGH SELF-ESTEEM	33
CHAPTER 5	**38**
BENEFIT OF HIGH SELF CONFIDENCE	38
CHAPTER 6	**47**
BENEFITS OF LOW SELF-CONFIDENCE	47
CHAPTER 7	**50**
THE BENEFITS OF LOW SELF-ESTEEM	50
Pros of Low Self Esteem:	*51*
Drawbacks of Low Self-Confidence	*52*
CHAPTER 8	**56**
9 TYPES OF SELF-ESTEEM AND THEIR CHARACTERISTICS	56

Ross Classification *58*

What's the difference between Self-Confidence and Self-Esteem? *61*

CHAPTER 9 .... **64**

8 SUGGESTIONS FOR CONDITIONING SELF-ESTEEM WHEN YOU HAVE DEPRESSION 64

CHAPTER 10 .... **71**

HOW TO IMPROVE YOUR SELF-ESTEEM: 12 POWERFUL TIPS 71

CHAPTER 11 .... **85**

10 METHODS FOR ENHANCING YOUR SELF-ESTEEM 85

Copyright © 2020 by Regina Williams

All rights reserved. No part of this publication may be reproduced, distributed, or transmitted in any form or by any means, including photocopying, recording, or other electronic or mechanical methods, without the prior written permission of the publisher, except in the case of brief quotations embodied in critical reviews and certain other non-commercial uses permitted by copyright law.

ISBN: 978-1-63750-256-3

Introduction

We all know that self-esteem, otherwise known as self-confidence, is an essential part of success.

It's time you stop losing opportunities and start investing in building your self-confidence and overcome self-doubt.

Inadequate self-esteem and self-confidence can leave people psychologically defeated or stressed out. Additionally, it may lead people to make bad options, fall into harmful relationships, or inability to make people attain their full potential.

Are concerned about changing your life and achieving your goals without the obstruction of your internal critics but with high sense of self-worth and confidence? This is the book for you!

An excessive amount of self-esteem, as exhibited in narcissistic personality disorder, could be off-putting to others, and may also harm personal relationships.

Self-esteem levels, at the extreme high and low ends of

the spectrum, can be dangerous, so ideally, you need to strike an equilibrium somewhere in the center; An authentic yet positive view of yourself is usually considered the perfect. But precisely, what is self-esteem? Where will it result from, and what impact does it have on our lives?

This book will give you the tools to understand self-esteem, self-confidence and teach you the techniques to master it effectively; you will learn how to stop the negative and paralysing self-talk and establish daily positive affirmations that will impact your subconscious mind and will improve your confidence.

In this book you will learn the types of self-esteem and their features, the methods of enhancing your self-worth, and many more!

After reading this book, you would simply be a new person with a changed heart and strong level of inner strength.

Chapter 1

What is Low Self-Esteem

Low self-esteem is seen as too little self-confidence, a state of feeling terrible about oneself. People who have low self-esteem often feel unlovable, uncomfortable, or incompetent.

Regarding experts *Morris Rosenberg and Timothy J. Owens*, who published Low Self-Esteem People: A Collective Portrait, people who have low self-esteem tend to be hypersensitive. They have a delicate sense of personality that can be wounded by others.

Furthermore, people who have low self-esteem are "hyper-vigilant and hyper-alert to signs of rejection, inadequacy, and rebuff," write Rosenberg and Owens. Often, individuals missing self-esteem see rejection and disapproval even though there isn't any. "The risk always lurks that they can make a blunder, use poor judgment, take action humiliating, expose (themselves) to ridicule, behave immorally, or contemptibly. Life, in every of its variety, poses on the ongoing danger to the self-esteem."

While everyone's self-esteem is susceptible to other folks, who may openly criticize them, ridicule them, or explain their flaws, I'd argue a sustained threat to each person's self-esteem lurks within. Rosenberg and Owens describe, "As observers of our very own behaviour, thoughts, and emotions, we not only register these phenomena in consciousness but also move judgement to them. Thus, we might be our most unfortunate critic, berating ourselves mercilessly whenever we find ourselves making one in judgement, forgetting might know about keep in mind, expressing ourselves awkwardly, breaking our most sacred guarantees to ourselves, dropping our self-control, performing childishly-in brief, behaving with techniques that people regret and could deplore."

This harsh inner critic, which *Dr. Robert Firestone* identifies as the *Critical Inner Tone of voice*, contributes to a poor perceived personal. Having a weak belief in oneself can have serious effects. *For instance, if someone feels that other folks don't like them, they will avoid relationships with others and are quicker to react defensively, cynically, or even lash out.* Rosenberg and Owen claim that "the type and level to which we connect to others is highly affected by our self-recognition, no matter their precision. Indeed, our self-recognition represent one of the most crucial foundations which our social behaviour is built on."

Furthermore, whenever we perceive ourselves adversely, whether we label ourselves uncomfortable, unlovable, obnoxious, timid, etc., it becomes increasingly more challenging to think that others may see us in a positive light. "The bottom line is that to have low self-esteem is to live a life of misery," concludes Rosenberg and Owen.

- **Conquering Low Self-Esteem**

The glad tidings are that it's entirely possible to overcome low self-esteem! You will find two critical components to combatting this negative self-image. The foremost is to **stop hearing your critical internal voice**. The second reason is to **start training self-compassion**.

- *Stop Hearing Your Internal Critic*

The critical internal tone of voice is that inner observer that hurtfully judges our thoughts and activities. This unpleasant inner critic continually nags us with a barrage of mental poison about ourselves and individuals all around us. It decimates our self-esteem constantly with thoughts like…

"You're ridiculous."

"Your body is fat."

"No one likes you."

"You ought to be quiet. Every time you chat, you merely make a fool of yourself."

"Why can't you end up like other folks?"

"You're worthless."

To be able to overcome low self-esteem, you must challenge this mental poison and endure your internal critic. On *PsychAlive*, we have a whole portion of articles, several *Webinars, and an ecourse* specialized in this subject matter. The first rung on the ladder is to identify when you begin thinking these types of mental poison about yourself. Then, you can choose not to pay attention to your inner critic's character assassinations or lousy advice. It could be beneficial to imagine how you'll feel if another person was saying these exact things for you; you'd probably feel angry and inform them to shut up or clarify they are wrong about you. Take this process in answering your inner critic.

One way to get this done is to jot down all your internal critic's criticisms using one side of a bit of paper. Then jot down a more practical and compassionate appraisal of yourself, on the other hand. *For instance, if you write a self-criticism like "You're ridiculous," you could then write, "I might struggle sometimes, but I am smart and competent in lots of ways."*

Challenging your inner critic helps stop the pity spiral that feeds into low self-esteem. When you understand the critical internal voice as a way to obtain your negative self-attacks, you can start to defy this inner critic and find out yourself for who you indeed are.

- ***Start Practicing Self-Compassion***

In lots of ways, the cure for self-criticism is self-compassion. Self-compassion is the radical practice of treating yourself just like a friend; it is an excellent way to create more confidence in yourself. Research shows that self-compassion is better still for your mental health than self-esteem.

Dr. Kristen Neff, who researches self-compassion, explains that self-compassion is not predicated on self-evaluation or judgement; instead, it is dependent on a positive attitude of kindness and acceptance toward yourself. While this might sound simple, treating yourself with compassion and sympathy may be challenging initially. However, you will establish more self-compassion as you practice it often.

Listed below are the three steps for practicing self-compassion:

1. Acknowledge and notice your hurts.

2. Be kind and caring in response to struggles.

3. Understand that imperfection is an area of every human's experience.

You'll find self-compassion exercises on *Dr. Kristen Neff's website*.

How to Develop Self-Confidence

Research into self-esteem shows that both low and high self-esteem can create emotional and sociable problems for folks. While high levels of self-esteem can be associated with narcissism. Lesser degrees of self-esteem can be related to social anxiety, insufficient confidence, and depression. The healthiest kind of self-confidence is "the moderate self-esteem that is situated more on valuing one's inherent worth as a person and less about comparing oneself to others." With this mindset, if your goal is to build up more self-confidence, it is best to concentrate on having high amounts of self-worth rather than high degrees of self-esteem.

Furthermore, to challenging your internal critic and exercising self-compassion, here are some other approaches for feeling better about yourself.

Stop Comparing You to ultimately Other People

Looking to increase your confidence by measuring yourself with others is an error. *Dr. Kristen Neff* clarifies, "Our competitive culture tells us we have to be special and above average to feel great about ourselves, but we can't all be above average at the same time. There is always someone richer, more appealing, or successful people than we are."

Whenever we evaluate ourselves predicated on external achievements, other people's perceptions and competitions, "our sense of self-worth bounce around like a ping-pong ball, rising and falling in lock-step with this latest success or failure." Social media only exacerbates this issue, as people post their picture-perfect occasions and shiny achievements, which we compare to your tarnished, flawed everyday lives.

Being able to create a healthy sense of confidence, we have to stop comparing ourselves to others. Rather than worrying about how exactly you measure to individuals around you, think about the kind of person you desire to be. Arranged goals and take activities that are constant with your values.

Surpass Your Own Moral Code

Self-confidence and self-esteem are designed on self-respect. If you live a life that is consistent with your principles, whatever they might be, you will respect yourself, feel well informed, and even do better in life. For instance, a report at the University of Michigan discovered that students "who based their self-esteem on internal sources-such to be a virtuous person or sticking with moral standards-were found to get higher grades and less inclined to use drugs and alcohol or even to develop eating disorders."

To feel great about yourself, it's important to have integrity and ensure that your activities match your words. For instance, if eating healthy and looking your very best are important ideals for you, you will feel better if you keep up a wholesome lifestyle. Whenever your activities don't match your words, you are more susceptible to self-attacks. The internal critic wants to explain these shortcomings. It is valuable to take into account your core concepts and act consistently with those beliefs if you are trying to improve your confidence.

Take Action Meaningful

As humans, we tend to feel great about ourselves whenever we do something significant, getting involved in activities that are bigger than ourselves and beneficial to others. That is an attractive strategy to use about building self-confidence and developing healthier degrees of self-esteem.

Studies also show that volunteering has an optimistic effect on how people experience themselves. Researcher Jennifer Crocker shows that you find "an objective that is bigger than the personal." When going after meaningful activities, it's essential to take into account what feels the most important to you. For a lot of, this might mean volunteering at a homeless shelter, tutoring children, getting involved in local politics, gardening with friends, etc. Follow the breadcrumbs of where you find meaning, and you'll find your self-esteem on the way.

Chapter 2

Why is Self-Esteem Important?

Self-esteem identifies a person's values about their well worth. Also, it is due to the emotions people experience that determines how they use their senses. Self-confidence is essential since it greatly influences people's options and decisions. Self-esteem acts as a motivational function, which makes it pretty much likely that individuals will look after themselves and explore their full potential.

People who have high self-esteem are also folks who are motivated to care for themselves and also to strive towards the fulfilment of personal goals and aspirations persistently. People who have lower self-esteem tend to disrespect themselves, also tend to let considerations slide and also to be less prolonged and resilient in conditions of conquering adversity. They could have the same types of goals as people who have higher self-esteem; however, they are usually less motivated to pursue them with their conclusion.

Self-esteem is somewhat an abstract idea; it's hard for someone who doesn't have it to learn what it might be like and own it. One of the ways that people who have lower self-esteem can start to understand what it might be to prefer having higher self-esteem is to consider how they could experience things they value in their lives.

For example, some people enjoy cars because vehicles are essential to them; these folks take excellent treatment of their vehicles. They make the right decisions about where you can park the automobile, how often to get it serviced, and exactly how they'll drive it. They could decorate the automobile and then show it off to other folks with satisfaction.

Self-esteem is similar to that, you look after yourself, like yourself, and feel pleased with yourself. When children believe they may be valuable and essential, they take proper care of themselves; they make the right decisions about themselves, which improves their value rather than break it down.

Sizes of Self-Esteem

High vs. Low Self-esteem

Self-esteem is regarded as occurring on the continuum, and therefore it is considered to efficiently vary in amount or magnitude from low to high across different individuals. Some individuals have higher self-esteem, while some have lower self-esteem. The variations between these folks are not apparent, but instead are evident only through assessment of their thoughts and emotions about their worthy of.

Proportionality of Self-Esteem: Self-esteem is also considered to vary in yet another way, which we may describe as proportionality or reasonableness. As it happens that not absolutely all cases of high self-esteem will be the same, some individuals with high self-esteem have attained that place predicated on some real accomplishments. They provide themselves credit to be in a position to meet new difficulties because they have had the opportunity to meet earlier problems. Their reasonable opinion of themselves is compared to the actual issues they have to conquer in life.

On the other hand, there are other folks whose high self-esteem seems extreme and away out of proportion with their real accomplishments and actions. These folks think well of themselves but cannot indicate any substantive past achievements, efforts, or options they have made, which would justify that high self-opinion to a good-minded observer. Their higher self-esteem is situated more on a feeling of entitlement than on any achievement. This entitled version of high self-esteem is known to be less psychologically healthy than the greater proportional variety of self-esteem, mainly because of the selfish and self-centred behaviour that will accompany the sense of entitlement. This variety of high self-esteem may also be referred to as "overly-inflated," indicating that it's extreme and out of percentage to real accomplishments and activities. In adults, this kind of self-esteem can be associated with Narcissism.

Just like self-esteem can be too much or "overly-inflated" compared to someone's achievements and actions, it may also be too low, or "under-inflated" as well. Often people who finish up having poor self-esteem already have fulfilled adversity and difficulties and treated others well and do have a basis for sense reasonable about themselves.

However, for various reasons, including an inclination towards depression, stress, or obsessive perfectionism, a habit of participating in cognitive distortions, or because they have been abused or exploited, they might not identify these achievements and activities as significant. They perceive themselves as failing woefully to meet an internalized and unreasonably high standard of goodness and therefore display surprisingly low self-esteem and related emotional stress when they cannot meet that internal standard. However, another observer would see them as deserving based on achievements and actions and also have difficulty understanding why exactly they feel so terrible about themselves.

Self-esteem is thus more difficult when compared to just high or low dimensions. It varies both in conditions of magnitude, and in requirements of its reasonableness when put next against achievements and activities. Parents wanting to foster healthy self-esteem in their children need to nurture and cultivate both these dimensions. The majority of this record will continue to spell out techniques parents could work to nurture their children's healthy self-esteem. Before describing these procedures, however, you want to clarify further why wholesome self-esteem, proportional to real success and behaviour and neither over-inflated nor under-inflated, is desired.

Chapter 3

Great Things about High Self-Esteem

Everyone desires to be happy, successful in life, and achieve their dreams. But what determines our accomplishments?

Numerous mental studies which were conducted over 50 years ago supports the data that, success in life relates to self-confidence. Self-confident people usually flourish in all spheres of life, and on the other hand, successful people routinely have a high degree of confidence.

Furthermore, psychological research reveals that self-confidence is vital for performance in virtually any activity and issues just as much as abilities. Confidence is essential to progressing Atlanta divorce Attorneys facet of our lives, yet many people battle to develop this quality. They regularly ask themselves if they're smart, attractive, or sufficient to be happy rather than stop fretting about that other folks may think about them.

Unfortunately, individuals who have low self-confidence find it hard to achieve success. If you have problems with poor self-esteem, you should take measures to overcome it to feel great about yourself and be the master of your life.

What's Self-Esteem and Why could it be Important?

Two qualities donate to self-confidence: **self-esteem and self-efficacy**. *Albert Bandura*, a psychologist at Stanford University or college, defines self-efficacy as people's values in their capabilities to get success in a particular situation that regulates how we think, feel, and behave.

Individuals who have plenty of self-confidence in their features consider difficult jobs as challenges to understand their skills rather than as threats they ought to avoid. Confidence enhances a person's inspiration to place much work in attaining his goals and get over numerous problems and temptations that test his / her willpower.

Self-esteem is our actual emotional emotions and views about ourselves, our self-worth, or personal value. It offers benefits about oneself, plus some emotional states - pride, shame, despair, and triumph. It impacts how exactly we think, act, and relate with other folks, and we can live our lives to your potentials. Self-Esteem determines how happy we are and has a primary bearing on our well-being.

High self-esteem makes a foundation for each positive experience in your daily life and can help you see positives sides of Atlanta divorce attorney's situation, complete a down economy, and appreciate memories. Having high self-esteem is essential for every area of one's life - it relates to all the good stuff that you can think of:

- better economic standing up
- good mental and physical health
- higher educational achievements
- happy personal relationships

- better career prospects

High self-esteem gives you the strength to consider the charge you will ever have, study from mistakes, and grow as a person.

10 Most Common Great Things About Having High Self-Esteem

1. You are more resilient to troubles and issues that are inevitable in life. Whenever your self-esteem is high, you find a way and skills to jump back the failing, learn from errors, and make modifications to enhance the situation and overcome the obstacles.

2. You are feeling happy and at ease with your daily life because you respect yourself, and others respect you.

3. You are feeling more motivated to attain your targets because high self-esteem enables you to be trusted by other folks and enhances your confidence in your ability to achieve success. Because of this, you are more motivated to

consider actions.

4. You love associations with friends and companions better and attract successful and confident people in your daily life, who assist you more for your positive energy.

5. You can accept the challenges because you are confident in your strengths and know you can master everything.

6. You perform better at any task, personal or related to your studies or your responsibility.

7. Your daily life is more exciting, make an effort to use every opportunity, and take dangers because you are feeling assured that you can flourish in everything and reach your goals.

8. You recognize that you don't have to be perfect, which means you feel less stressed. You are certainly not scared to make bad decisions because you realize that anyone can cause errors, and its okay.

9. You will be yourself and do need to adapt your behaviour, values, and views to meet anticipations of other folks. You aren't concerned that other people can disagree with your opinions or behaviour. You don't need the approval of other people. You that it's impossible to please everyone, and that means you do what you take into account to be right.

10. You are successful in every sphere of life. You respect yourself and respect everyone around you. You make an excellent sociable image that plays a part in your individual and social development.

They are only a few of the fantastic benefits of high self-esteem, but there are a lot more reasons why high self-esteem is essential for keeping a balanced lifestyle. Confident folks have the energy to conquer the world; they may be adored by everyone and inspire other people to check out their examples.

They face challenges of life, take risks and seize

opportunities, never quit, and flourish in everything they are doing - in school, in social and personal life, and at the job. Even if indeed they fail, they optimistically see themselves and their lives so they respect themselves, and because of this, they are recognized by others.

Developing self-confidence: Self-confidence is a superb skill, and it could be learned and perfected by anyone precisely like some other skill. You merely have to trust in yourself, and other folks will have confidence in you as well as your very existence will completely change for the better. If you have problems with low self-confidence or self-esteem, you should try to develop these features in yourself.

You can find special techniques that you should practice every day, and you're sure to become a self-confident person everyone will admire.

Quick Easy Methods to Build Self-Esteem

Gain control of yourself: Don't be too critical, comparing yourself to other people. People are different, and every life has its value. Make a summary of your positive characteristics and advantages and have confidence in yourself. Understand that you are unique, and you truly deserve to feel great about yourself.

Look after your feelings and figure out how to manage panic, stress, frustration, anger, dread better. When you understand how to handle these emotions, you'll also figure out how to take charge of your ideas and behaviour.

Don't be considered a complainer: Stop concentrating on complications and problems in your daily life; Instead, focus on their solutions and think about making positive changes. Be appreciative for all those good stuff in your everyday life, your loved ones, friends, as well as your achievements.

Identify your realistic targets/vision: Take efforts to accomplish your targets and gauge the progress you make. Make the set of your accomplishments that you will be proud of.

Enjoy positive human relationships and remove negative folks from your daily life: Spend additional time with people who fill you up with positive feelings and help you increase your self-esteem.

There is absolutely no magic solution that can enhance your self-esteem and cause you to a far more confident person simultaneously. You must learn to feel great about yourself and become comfortable with the individual that you will be, and it requires lots of time, patience, and commitment.

Now you understand developing self-esteem, so start making steps to changing your daily life right now, and you'll be amazed at results.

Chapter 4
Importance of High Self-Esteem

The advantages of wholesome self-esteem are numerous. Children who have high self-esteem come to value themselves and think of themselves as worthwhile partners and able problem solvers. They create a healthy balance of liking who they are but also recognizing that we now have ways they can continue steadily to grow and also to develop.

With wholesome self-esteem, children believe that they have positive characteristics and skills they can provide to other folks, plus they also feel these are worth being loved and accepted by others, including relatives and buddies. They feel fundamental worth of their fair share of resources like food, shelter, love, time, respect, and dignity. Children with healthy self-esteem will be happy to make and keep positive friends, and also to persevere in working through difficult situations that occur in relationships, they'll see challenging conditions as opportunities to try something new, even if they are not entirely successful; Because they like themselves and believe they are worth being looked after by others, they are not as likely than people who have lower self-esteem in which to stay abusive or exploitive situations.

Also, they are much more likely to look after themselves physically and emotionally, and also to persist in difficult and effortful pursuits such as completing their education or mastering an occupation.

In contrast, a minimal (or reduced) self-esteem is commonly associated with an increase in adverse outcomes. Youngsters with low self-esteem do not feel like they have many positive, valuable characteristics and could feel ashamed, guilty, sad, or angry about themselves. As a result of this, they may think that they don't deserve basic things such as food, shelter, love, time, respect, or dignity from others. They could behave in negative; self-defeating techniques finish up confirming their poor opinion of themselves. *For instance, they could convince themselves they aren't smart enough to pass a math test. Because they believe they don't have the capacity to earn a good grade, they don't put much energy or effort into finding your way through the test*. They could also anxiously dwell on thoughts about how badly they will perform. Then they fail the test, more consequently of insufficient sustained study effort, and anxious preoccupation than due to a genuine lack of ability. This failure then is interpreted incorrectly, but with great emotional "truth" weight as further proof that they are indeed bad at math. Further efforts at learning math are then discouraged in the wake of the failure experience. This type of negative feedback cycle of self-defeating thoughts and behaviour is sometimes referred to as a self-fulfilling prophecy.

Youngsters with poor self-esteem are less inclined to be happy, and much more likely to have emotional and public problems than are their higher self-esteem peers. Lower self-esteem children are less willing to persevere through difficult situations because they presume they cannot succeed under challenging circumstances; therefore, give up too early. They might be more likely to be victimized or exploited by others, because they don't highly believe they deserve to be treated well, or because they believe they lack the features essential to better or escape off their situation.

Children with excessively inflated self-esteem predicated on a feeling of narcissistic entitlement rather than on genuine fulfilment. Such children may complacently view themselves as more perfect and more worth to use specific resources than other children, with the effect that they run arrogantly. They could dismiss and therefore fail to reap the benefits of constructive interpersonal criticism, which other children would use with their advantage to identify areas for productive growth or change. They could exhibit "externalization," which is to state that they assume incorrectly that the failings of other folks cause problems they experience, and they haven't any responsibility to improve. Sometimes children with inflated self-esteem will resort to bullying others because they believe they must be permitted to judge others, and also to treat them nonetheless they wish.

Children who do not grow out of the immature, entitled pattern will most likely continue to have less success than their genuinely high self-esteem counterparts, at least in regards to their ability to create lasting and emotionally satisfying intimate relationships.

Chapter 5

Benefit of High Self Confidence

Women and men across the world have problems with low self-confidence, but it generally does not have to remain that way. Studies show a girl's self-confidence peaks around age nine but wane with adolescence.

In this chapter, we're uncovering a few key ways high self-confidence can change your daily life, getting you better than previously compared to that confident and guaranteed 9-year-old that's still inside.

1. <u>Criticism Loosens Its Hold</u>: Criticism has many encounters; sometimes, it's constructive, *as whenever a manager gently informs you of openings in your performance that can result in a stronger result when addressed*. When given in this framework, criticism is often helpful and healthy.

Generally, criticism appears like an awful side-effect of low self-confidence. It can change spouses against one another, tear family apart, and damage relationships.

When we absence self-confidence in ourselves, it becomes quite challenging to trust in others, and because of this, we can create unobtainable ideals that even those closest to us can't reach. When you adopt a way of thinking of high self-confidence, you'll readjust your outlook, giving yourself, as well as your family members some freedom to make errors but still receive love.

2. <u>Stress Becomes More Manageable</u>: According to a recently available survey, over fifty percent of working adults are worried about the degrees of stress in their lives. From deadlines to family responsibilities and every result in among, it may become easy to feel overwhelmed by all we must juggle.

When we absence confidence inside our ability to execute, that weight shifts from merely challenging to all-encompassing and frequently unbearable. Alternatively, high self-confidence helps us muster the power and determination to handle even the most stressful situation head-on.

From headaches and hypertension to libido reduction

and depression, stress can play a reasonably hard role on our anatomies, wearing them right down to the idea of exhaustion. Choosing to approach stressful situations with self-assured courage and tenacity can change even the steepest mountain into a scalable molehill.

3. <u>You can express yourself more clearly</u>: Will there be anything in your daily life you would like to try if failing weren't so glaringly a choice? Are you scratching to state something but aren't sure how?

The answer does not have to be as dramatic as, "Let me attempt skydiving."

Maybe there is a broken friendship you would like to patch; nevertheless, you aren't confident enough to try again. Perhaps you're considering a profession change, but don't believe you have what must be done to return to college or start once more in the labour force. That boulder standing up in the right path? Probably, it's on your esteem.

High self-confidence helps you grab the items you want, require the thing you need, and speak your brain with an increase of surety. Studies show that lots of people, especially ladies in the labour force, are hesitant to negotiate for a much better situation. People frequently have a propensity to concentrate on the needs of others over their own. Building high self-confidence helps you switch that attention a bit more inward, providing yourself the increase you will need to make that crucial first move.

4. <u>Your Relationships Are Healthier</u>: With high self-confidence, you will not only treat yourself better, but you're also better in a position to build the healthy, strong interactions you want in your daily life. If you are alert to what you do and do not wish and better ready to articulate those feelings, you attract the type of positive energy you produce.

Because of this, you're also keenly alert to those romantic relationships that are more toxic than uplifting and are better equipped to eliminate yourself from them if required. From abusive spouses to jealous, spiteful "frenemies," you can spot individuals whose behaviour has been exacerbating your emotions of self-doubt and loneliness.

There's a primary hyperlink between abuse (in its every form) and low self-confidence, though leaving isn't always as cut and dried out as merely cutting off ties.

If you or someone you understand is within an abusive romantic relationship, the *Countrywide Domestic Violence Hotline* offers a helpful Security Plan to show you toward freedom. Here are articles that target rebuilding finances after escaping an abusive romantic relationship, providing tips about budgeting, building credit, and getting back to the workforce.

5. <u>Setbacks Don't Keep You Down</u>: Despite having high self-confidence, you will not be immune to all or any of life's inevitable ebbs and moves. The truth is that despite having all the self-esteem in the world, you will likely still experience setbacks, disappointments, and failures. You can get knocked down briefly, but you will have the power to reunite up and continue.

With low self-confidence, even the tiniest obstacle can

feel just like an enormous blow. When that is the case, every day becomes challenging. Choosing to handle every situation with self-assurance helps to ensure that regardless of what hands you're dealt, you'll bravely acknowledge it. This also provides you that extra confidence enhances you will need to jump fearlessly into those big, new, and yet, sometimes scary, unknowns.

Drawbacks of high self-confidence

Mental anxiousness or frustration: When you don't like or approve of the main person you're home with every day, your anxiousness and depression are natural consequences.

Heavy self-criticism: A habitual condition of dissatisfaction with yourself leads to exaggerating the magnitude of errors or behaviours. Additionally, you start struggling to forgive yourself.

Hypersensitivity to criticism: If you feel attacked regularly, you will close yourself off to constructive criticism. Which inevitably means stunted development and progress.

<u>Inability to accept compliments</u>: Because you can't take criticism doesn't mean you can receive compliments. It looks as though people are either lying or out to get you truly

<u>Chronic indecision</u>: A concern with making mistakes leads to inaction, and inaction on your part leaves both responsibility and success to others. The lack of self-trust if you don't like yourself, likely, your opinions aren't going to matter for you, and if you don't trust yourself, you won't do something by yourself, or in the direction of your dreams.

<u>Perfectionism</u>: This moves hand-in-hand with chronic indecision, as both are rooted in a concern with making mistakes, and for that reason being unaccepted. Perfectionism leads to continuous frustration, and frequently underachievement when recognized perfection isn't achieved.

<u>Self-neglect</u>: It is individual nature to care for what we should love and overlook whatever we don't like. Your

patterns of self-care, nourishment, sleep, exercise, cultural interactions - are a representation of your self-esteem.

Eating disorders: If you look into the mirror and don't like what you observe, inside or away, where do you begin to change that understanding? Sadly, food is usually a pawn in the fight to attain self-love. It is "there," it does not have any opinion, and it could be managed and manipulated. And since "in charge," even briefly, can give food to dependence on empowerment for a person with low self-esteem.

Addictions: When the pain of coping with oneself is too much to carry, habits are given birth to drown the pain. What pretends to be always a "friend" initially quickly becomes a brutal foe. The addict already does not have any self-confidence or willpower to endure it; therefore, the risk only deepens.

Failure to persevere and overcome hurdles when you have low self-esteem, problems aren't just issues; they include intimidation, a chance to fail.

Loss of wish: of all drawbacks of low self-esteem, none

could become more informing or devastating than the increased loss of hope. Low self-esteem feeds over-all negativity about life, and frequently an inability to take pleasure from it or expect anything from it.

Chapter 6

Benefits of Low Self-Confidence

1. Minimizes Prospect of Failure

If confidence is absent, you will be lazy and place low objectives for yourself. You're less inclined to take risks so that it reduces your likelihood of experiencing failing.

2. Predictability

By not being confident, you can predict how people will treat you. You obtain it when people don't acknowledge you or like being around you. Because of this, you don't have to try too much or released a great deal of effort to build up relationships.

3. Receiving Attention

When you have a minimal level of self-confidence, you appear unsure of yourself and can be regarded as being needy. This compels visitors to want to look after you, build you up, and cause you to feel better. You obtain the attention you will possibly not have received usually.

4. Fitting In

Because you have low self-confidence, you're not going to be arrogant around people. Because of this, people will be helpful to you. Perhaps the majority of your family or friends will be the same way, which means this provides you ways to easily fit into socially.

As you can see, there are several benefits to having a minimal level of self-confidence. Once you come with a dependency, compulsion, or disorder of some kind, and you're not prepared to improve, you're getting something positive out to be that way. You genuinely get negative pleasure from it. You're benefiting in a poor, somewhat manipulative way that doesn't last, even if it's unconscious (and it usually), it's essential to notice that others around you will reap the benefits of your low self-confidence as well. *For example, your lover can feel better about themselves by firmly taking treatment of you. Your manager can hire you for lower-income because you'll feel "lucky" to have the job.*

People can help you to do things they need you to do because they know you won't say "no."

Mindful or unconscious, people will benefit from you!

Chapter 7
The Benefits of Low Self-Esteem

A lot of individuals tell me I have to lower my self-esteem in the service of modesty, credibility, and protecting the sensibilities of those around me. I want to heed that advice and become a team player, but I'm also plagued with rounds of rationality that are keeping me from causing this to be an improvement to my personality.

Before I do anything drastic in life, such as evolving into someone who thinks less of himself for the well-being of others, I love to do a benefits and drawbacks list. I'll focus on the benefits of thinking an excessive amount of myself.

It feels great! Regularly! It increases my testosterone; it boosts my performance for the most part things. Technology agrees that higher testosterone makes muscle development easier. I take more danger. (That is admittedly a combined bag.)

Cockiness comes with an aphrodisiac influence on some. (You understand who you are.) Now for the downside of thinking an excessive amount of myself, I take more dangers than I probably should. Higher testosterone raises cancer risks.

Pros of Low Self Esteem:

Cockiness (until I get malignancy anyway), I see my inflated sense of self-worth as more of a technique for happiness when compared to a flaw. And by that After all, I understand how to dial-back my self-esteem, but I choose never to.

There's no such thing as the right degree of self-esteem. Everyone who interacts with you'll have a different notion of how much is too much for you. Therefore, I intentionally err privately of too much. The vast benefits outweigh the expenses.

Take into account that I've succeeded in several fields where I had formed no identifiable skill before starting, including cartooning, the speaking circuit, and writing books experienced I cultivated a far more socially acceptable degree of self-esteem I wouldn't have attempted some of those challenges.

I've failed in my own life and my career about ten times more regularly than I've succeeded, but my artificially high sense of self-esteem allows me personally to quickly jump back again and keep punching until something lucky happens. Some of you'll be quick to indicate the difference between calm inner-confidence and as an arrogant dick on multiple websites. But if you believe high self-esteem can be masked, you almost certainly don't know very well what it is. As soon as you are feeling high self-esteem, you lose the filtration system. Entirely only, if you think you need to cover your high self-esteem, you don't have high self-esteem. That's how self-esteem works.

Drawbacks of Low Self-Confidence

Mental anxiousness or stress when you don't like or approve of the main person you are home with every day; stress and anxiety and depression are natural consequences.

Heavy self-criticism: A habitual condition of

dissatisfaction with yourself leads to exaggerating the magnitude of errors or behaviours. Additionally, you become struggling to forgive yourself.

Hypersensitivity to criticism: if you feel attacked regularly, you will close yourself off to constructive criticism. Which inevitably means stunted development and progress.

Inability to accept compliments Because you can't take criticism doesn't mean you can receive compliments. It looks as though people are either lying or out to get you truly.

Chronic indecision: A concern with making mistakes leads to inaction. And inaction on your part leaves both responsibility and success to others.

The lack of self-trust; if you don't like yourself, likely, your opinions aren't going to matter for you. And if you don't trust yourself, you won't do something by yourself or in the direction of your dreams.

Perfectionism: This runs hand-in-hand with chronic indecision, as both are rooted in a concern with making mistakes, and for that reason being unaccepted. Perfectionism leads to continuous frustration, and frequently underachievement when recognized perfection isn't gained.

Self-Neglect: It is individual nature to care for what we should love and overlook whatever we don't like. Your patterns of self-care, nourishment, sleep, exercise, cultural interactions - are a representation of your self-esteem.

Eating disorders: If you look into the mirror and don't like what you observe, inside or away, where do you begin to change that understanding? Sadly, food is usually a pawn in the fight to attain self-love. It is "there," it does not have any opinion, and it could be managed and manipulated. And since "in charge," even briefly, can give food to dependence on empowerment for a person with low self-esteem.

Addictions: When the pain of coping with oneself is too much to carry, habits are given birth to drown the pain. What pretends to be always a "friend" initially quickly becomes a brutal foe. The addict already does not have any self-confidence or willpower to endure it; therefore, the risk only deepens.

Failure to persevere and overcome hurdles When you have low self-esteem, problems aren't just issues; they include intimidation, a chance to fail.

Loss of wish: of all drawbacks of low self-esteem, none could become more informing or devastating than the increased loss of wish. Low self-esteem feeds over-all negativity about life, and frequently an inability to take pleasure from it or expect anything from it.

Chapter 8
9 Types of Self-Esteem and their Characteristics

The types of self-esteem can be classified into several levels based on the most known and used models: *Hornstein's and Ross's* - Self-esteem is the gratitude and esteem that someone has towards himself which is vitally important to build a good standard of living and become successful both individually and professionally.

Self-esteem is the available innate in every individual, from birth, and it is changing our lives.

Classification of types of self-esteem: the nine levels

The first five types we present, participate in *Hornstein's classification* and the last three to *Ross's*.

Hornstein classify the types of self-esteem as the steady or unstable, it lasts with time, whether its high or low

1. High and constant self-esteem

This kind could correspond with the firm or high self-esteem since people who have this kind of self-esteem aren't influenced by what negatively happens around them. Also, the guy can defend his perspective in a relaxed way, plus they thrive as time passes without collapsing.

2. High and unstable self-esteem

These folks are also seen as high self-esteem; however, not by maintaining it as time passes. They don't often have enough tools to cope with stressful environments plus they have a tendency to destabilize them, so they don't accept failure nor do they accept opposing positions to theirs

3. Steady and low self-esteem

These folks are seen as an underestimating, that is, they cannot do what they propose. Alternatively, they are incredibly hesitant and dread making errors, so they'll always seek the support of someone else. Nor do they battle for their factors of view, being that they are generally appreciated inadequately.

4. Unstable and low self-esteem

We're able to say that individuals who have this self-esteem are those who choose to go unnoticed all the time and who think they cannot get anything. Alternatively, they're usually very private and influenced and decide never to face anyone even if indeed they know that your partner is not right.

5. Inflated self-esteem

People with this kind of self-esteem are seen as having a robust personality and thinking themselves much better than individuals around them. Therefore, they never pay attention or pay any focus on them. They also tend to blame others in stressful situations and also have a massive ego. They cannot right their errors or criticize themselves. They may be seen as being very materialistic and superficial.

Ross Classification

Relating to Ross, an individual can have collapsed, vulnerable, and robust self-esteem.

1. Collapsed or low self-esteem

Individuals who have it do not usually appreciate themselves; this leads them never to feel great in their life. It makes them excessively sensitive from what others may say about them, so if it's negative, it'll harm them, and if it's positive, it'll increase their self-esteem.

If an adolescent exhibits this kind of self-esteem in senior high school, he might be the sufferer of bullying or bullying by his classmates and could even be excluded.

2. Vulnerable or regular self-esteem

In this type, the individual has a good self-concept, but his self-confidence is fragile when confronted with adverse situations such as the increased loss of someone you care about, not getting what he desires or proposes. This will lead him to produce defence mechanisms to avoid this kind of situation or have to make decisions since he fears mistakes and doing things wrong.

3. Strong or elevated self-esteem

It includes having a graphic and self-concept of oneself,

strong enough so that any mistake that is manufactured is unable to influencing self-esteem. People who have this self-esteem aren't scared to make errors and have tendency to overflow optimism, humility, and pleasure.

How will you know the exact type of self-esteem you possess? Self-esteem is formed even as we grow because of our romantic relationship with ourselves and with the surroundings and individuals around us.

Many factors influence the kind of self-esteem you have:

- *Relatives and buddies*

Our parents will be accountable for building our self-esteem from birth. If they don't have it at heart, they can adversely affect the labels or feedback they provide us when they address us: "you are ridiculous" or "you are a disobedient child" are some typically common examples.

As the kid develops, their self-esteem will be strengthened or weakened predicated on these labels, which their parents will put their teachers and friends.

- *Range of goals and objectives*

Take pleasure from good self-esteem is something significant that must exist inside our life. Getting a few of them gives us the confidence we need and also boost the positive perception, which will positively impact.

- *The attention that is received*

Being accepted and well known by individuals all around us also helps us to build up a kind of self-esteem in cases like this of high type. Alternatively, being desired by someone you value is also another component to consider, and that will assist build self-esteem.

What's the difference between Self-Confidence and Self-Esteem?

Self-confidence identifies the goal(s) a person proposes and their capability to accomplish them, while self-esteem is understood as a comprehensive assessment a person makes of himself.

How do we improve our self-esteem?

When you have low or regular self-esteem and want to boost it, below are a few tips that you can start to use in your daily life.

- **Love yourself:** Caring for oneself is among the best drugs which exist to increase self-esteem. If we only take a look at our shortcomings and what we should do and not do properly, we will live disappointed and frustrated with ourselves. Therefore, we must pay more focus on the ones that make us special and unique, which also offers us great to do.

- **Don't be a perfectionist:** Perfection will not exist; therefore, there will be something that people have no idea how to do flawlessly well. Being extremely critical won't benefit us and can impede our self-esteem and our love for ourselves.

- **Take failures constructively:** Many people make mistakes, we shouldn't be scared of making mistakes either, because if we do not make errors, we can't ever learn properly. Errors must be observed as resources of learning rather than as personal episodes.

- **Collection of realistic goals:** We must have the ability to get our goals together, goals that are viable and people can handle, both in the short and long-term. If it's not done in this manner, it'll only create pain, and we will never be pleased with ourselves.

- **Feel proud:** We should be pleased with what we are and what we have achieved in our lives since it has been the fruits of our work and commitment.

Chapter 9

8 Suggestions for Conditioning Self-Esteem when You have Depression

"Depression often distorts thinking, making a once-confident person feel insecure, negative and self-loathing," said *Deborah Serani, Ph.D*, a clinical psychologist and writer of the publication Coping with Depression.

Recent positive or natural thoughts become "I am incompetent," "I suck at everything," or "I hate myself,'" according to clinical psychologist *Dean Parker, Ph.D.* (Alternatively, "High self-esteem is associated with certain positive cognitions or values, such as 'I am good,' 'I am successful,' [or] 'I am valuable to others,'" he said. While low self-esteem may be deeply rooted, you can begin chipping away at the layers of loathing. Every day, you can take part in a task that enhances your self-esteem. Below, *Serani and Parker* talk about their tips about conditioning self-esteem, whether it's in as soon as or higher time.

1. <u>Cope with dysfunctional considering</u>: "Research demonstrates negative consideration as the linchpin accountable for leaving low self-esteem," Serani said depression also colors your world. "Depression corrodes view and considering styles," she said. Mental poison becomes destructive, causing you to be vulnerable to poor decisions and abusive situations, she said.

Parker likened this routine to a poor mp3 that "repeatedly says one's failures and self-doubts until they feel defeated and find out no wish or future." Dealing with these corrosive cognitions is crucial. An essential strategy is to research your ideas for precision. Serani suggested requesting these three questions:

"What evidence helps my thinking?

Would others say this holds about me?

Will feeling this way make me feel great about myself or bad about myself?"

This also contains replacing mental poison with positive ones. But, as Parker underscored, this doesn't mean repeating vacant affirmations; rather, it's about creating and using factual and significant self-statements.

The truth is that everyone has strengths and weaknesses. Having good self-esteem means taking and appreciating all of your edges. As *Psych Central's creator, John Grohol, Psy.D*, noted in this piece on self-esteem: People who have good and healthy self-esteem can feel great about themselves for who they are, appreciate their well worth, and take satisfaction in their capabilities and accomplishments. Also, they acknowledge that while they're not perfect and also have faults, those faults don't play a mind-boggling or irrationally significant role in their lives or their self-image (how you observe yourself).

2. <u>Journal</u>: Keeping mental poison in your mind only makes them bigger, Parker said. Journaling about these thoughts brings them right down to size, he said. Also, it helps you start to see the good stuff that can be found in your world.

Thus, besides, to list the mental poison, Parker suggested saving the strengths you will ever have, such as your wellbeing or family members.

3. <u>Seek positive support</u>: "Encircle yourself with people who celebrate your advantages, not your weaknesses," Serani said. Doing this not only feels good, but it additionally "helps solidify positive considerations," she said.

4. <u>Create visible cues</u>: Visible cues provide perspective and help you curb negative self-talk, Serani said. For example, she suggested departing positive records around your home and office and keeping inspiring estimates on your desktop.

5. <u>Start the day with a lift</u>: "Find books, calendars, and websites that are uplifting and uplifting for you," Parker said. Or start your entire day with a dosage of laughter, he said. (Laughter heals.) Facebook also offers funny memes you can follow, he said. While they could appear simple, these daily gestures are yet another way to make a supportive environment.

6. <u>Soothe yourself</u>: Both Serani and Parker pressured

the need for nurturing yourself, even though this is the very last thing you think you are worthy of or wish to accomplish. (Actually, that's when it's especially vital.)

"Feed your brain, body, and soul with techniques that makes you feel special," Serani said. These ways don't have to be grand (and overpowering). *For example, you may carve out the amount of time in your entire day for silence and stillness, she said. (Even several minutes' work, she added.) You may enjoy simple conveniences like a "hot sit down elsewhere, a beautiful track or a vibrant sunset," she said. Or you may "celebrate what you currently have rather than what you wish."*

7. <u>Discover and go after your passions</u>: When you're depressed as well as your self-esteem feels as though it's sinking daily, it's easy to overlook your passions. Parker recommended readers take time to "write a summary of things you used to like to do and halted doing along with things you always wished to do but haven't done yet."

He gave the exemplary case of a customer who

believed she wouldn't total anything and regularly compared herself to her successful friends. When Parker first asked about her passions, she couldn't identify any. Parker recommended she have a closer look and contemplate her positive characteristics and passions. After writing these down, she recognized she wished to become a fitness expert. Now she's taking programs and working toward her qualification. Identifying and going after her enthusiasm has boosted her self-confidence and given her a larger purpose.

8. <u>Redefine failing, and keep attempting</u>: When you have low self-esteem, it's common to think about yourself as a complete and utter failure. But failing is part of success, Parker said. Failing doesn't characterize you as a person or determine your self-worth.

When Parker coached Little league, he'd show his players that he didn't care if indeed they made mistakes on the field. What he does value was that they were swinging and lacking rather than merely standing there.

You will find countless stories of individuals persevering despite facing multiple rejections. Think about any article writer, scientist, designer, or performer. Everyone has confronted rejection at various factors in their lives.

As Parker said, "There's no assurance that all you do will bring positive opinions. All you have to is one indicator of success." For example, "engaging in one university out of 10 still enables you to be successful", he said. "Seize the positive declaration," he said. Quite merely, concentrate on the positive responses, and continue.

Conditioning your self-esteem isn't secure. But these useful pointers can show you in starting the procedure. If you believe your self-worth sis shattered, utilize a therapist to develop it right back up. It's never too past due to feeling great about yourself.

Chapter 10

How to Improve Your Self-Esteem: 12 Powerful Tips

1. Say No to your internal critic

An excellent spot to focus on raising your self-esteem is by learning the way to handle and also to replace the voice of your inner critic.

We all come with an inner critic. It could spur you to get things done or even to do what to gain approval from individuals in your daily life. But at precisely the same time, it'll drag your self-esteem down.

This inner voice whispers or shouts destructive thoughts in you. Thoughts such as:

- You are lazy and sloppy to work.

- You aren't proficient at your job whatsoever, and someone will physique that out and throw you out.

- You are worse or uglier than your friend/coworker/partner.

You don't have to accept this, though; you can find ways to reduce that critical tone of voice and also to replace it with an increase of helpful thoughts. You can transform how you view yourself.

- One way to take action is simply to state stop whenever the critic pops up in your thoughts.

- You can do this by developing a stop-word or stop-phrase.

As the critic says something - in your thoughts - shout: STOP! Or use the best: No, no, no, we aren't going there! Or think of a term or word that you want that halts idea driven by the internal critic.

Then refocus your ideas to something more constructive. Like planning what you would like to eat for supper or your strategy for another soccer game. Over time it also helps too much to find improved ways to motivate yourself than hearing your inner critic.

2. Use healthier inspiration habits

To help make the inner critic less effective and ultimately increase your self-esteem that definitely helps to have healthy inspiration habits there are several techniques I've used to displace and fill much of the spot that the internal critic once held in my brain, they are:

Remind yourself of the vast benefits: A straightforward but powerful way to motivate yourself and also to keep that inspiration up daily is to jot down the deeply experienced benefits you get, new route or reaching an objective.

- Such as engaging in better form and having more energy for your children and individuals close to you, or making additional money and during that, having the ability to travel with the love you will ever have and experience beautiful new things collectively.

- Whenever your list is performed, then save it and put it someplace where you will notice it every day, *for example, in your workspace or on your fridge.*

- Refocus on doing everything you really enjoy to do. When you truly, enjoy doing something, then your motivation to achieve that thing will come reasonably automatically. When you truly want something in life, then it also becomes simpler to drive through any internal resistance you are feeling.

- If you lose your inspiration, consider: Am I doing what I must say I wish to accomplish? If not and when possible, then refocus and begin focusing on those essential things instead.

- Once you've used your stop-word or phrase, concentrate on one of the techniques. As time passes, it will turn into a habit as well as your internal critic will pop-up much less often.

3. Have a 2-minute self-appreciation break

This habit is quite simple and fun, and if you may spend just two minutes onto it every day for per month, then it can make a big difference.

Here's what you do:

- Take a breath, decelerate, and have yourself this question: what exactly are three things I could appreciate about myself?

Several examples which have to appear when I've used to the exercise are:

- Help several people every day through what I write.

- Could make people laugh and forget about their troubles.

- I am very thoughtful and caring as it pertains to our pet cats.

These exact things don't need to be significant, maybe that you listened entirely for a few moments to a person who needed it today. That you required a wholesome walk or bicycle trip after work, rather than being lazy. That you will be a nurturing and kind person in many situations.

These brief breaks do not only build self-esteem over

time but can also turn a poor mood around and reload you with a lot of positive energy again.

4. Jot down three things at night that you can appreciate about yourself

That is a variation of the habit above, and combining each of them can be extra powerful for just two boosts in self-esteem each day, or you might choose to use this variance by the end of your entire day when you have some leisure time for you to ultimately spare.

Everything you do is to consider the question from the last section:

What exactly are three things I could appreciate about myself? Jot down your answers each night in a journal crafted from paper or on your computer/smart telephone.

An excellent extra advantage of writing it down is that after a couple of weeks, you can go through all the answers to remain positive and get a good self-esteem increase and change in perspective on times when you might need it the most.

5. Do the right thing

When you do what you deep down think is the right move to make when you raise and strengthen your self-esteem.

It could be a little thing like waking up from the sofa and visiting the gym. Maybe it's to be understanding rather than judgmental in times or even to stop being concerned or feeling sorry for yourself and concentrate on the opportunities and gratitude for what you truly have.

It isn't always easy to do. Or to know very well what the right thing is. But keeping a concentrate on it and carrying it out as best you can make a huge difference both in the results you get as well as for how you see yourself. One tip that means it is simpler to stay constant with doing the right thing is to attempt to have a few such activities in the morning. Such as providing someone a go with, eating a wholesome breakfast, and training.

6. Replace the perfectionism

Few thought habits can be as harmful in lifestyle as perfectionism. It could paralyze you from taking action because you feel so afraid of not living up for some standard, and that means you procrastinate, and you don't get the results you want. This can make your self-esteem kitchen sink, or you do something but should never be or very hardly ever content with what you accomplished as well as your performance.

Therefore, your opinion and emotions about yourself are more and more negative as well as your motivation to do this plummets.

How will you overcome perfectionism?

A couple of things that helped me are:

- Go for sufficiency: When you shoot for excellence, then that always winds up in a task or an activity never being completed. So; go once and for all enough instead. Don't utilize it as a justification to slack off. But merely realize that there is undoubtedly something called sufficient, so when you are there, then you are completed.

- <u>Understand that buying into myths of excellence will harm you and individuals in your daily life</u>: This simple reminder that life is nothing like in a movie, a track, or a publication can be a good fact check once you are daydreaming of excellence. Because actuality can clash with your anticipations when they may be out of the world and damage or even possibly business lead to the finish of relationships, careers, projects, etc.

7. <u>Handle errors and failures in a far more positive way</u>: If you go beyond your safe place, if you make an effort to accomplish whatever is meaningful, then you will stumble and fall on the way. Which is OK. It is normal. It is what folks that do something that genuinely mattered did throughout all age groups. Even if we don't always hear about any of it just as much as we hear about their successes.

So; understand that. When you stumble try out this:

- Be your own closest friend - Instead of defeating yourself up, consider: How would my friend/mother or father support me and help me in this example? Then do things and speak to yourself as she or he would. It maintains you from dropping into a pit of despair and allows you to become more constructive following the first preliminary pain of a blunder or failure begins to dissipate.

- Find the upside - Another way to become more constructive in this type of situation is to concentrate on optimism and opportunities. So consider: what exactly can I gain from this? And what's one opportunity I can find in this example? This will help you change your point of view and ideally not strike the same bump just a little further later on.

8. Be kinder towards other folks

If you are compassionate towards others, you have a tendency to treat and kindly think of yourself too, and how you treat other people is the way they tend to treat you over time. So; concentrate on being kind in your lifestyle.

For example:

- You need to be there and listen as you let someone vent.

- Hold up the entranceway for another person.

- Let someone into the lane while traveling.

- Encourage a pal or a member of the family when these are uncertain or unmotivated.

- Take a short while helping someone out in a practical way.

- Talk about what has helped you in a hard situation on the sociable press, a podcast, or your blog.

9. Try something new

When you try something new when you solve your problem in a little or more significant way and go beyond your safe place, in that case, your opinion of yourself rises. You might not do whatever you did in a great or smart way. Nevertheless, you at least tried rather than sitting on the hands and doing nothing, which is something to understand about yourself, and it can benefit you stand out as you escape a rut.

So; go beyond your safe place regularly. Don't expect anything, inform yourself that you'll try something out and then down the road, you can do a similar thing some more times and improve your performance.

10. Stop dropping into the assessment trap

When comparing your daily life and what you have to other people's lives and what they have, then you have a destructive habit on the hands because you can never win. There's always someone who has more or is preferable to you at something in the world.

So; replace that habit with something better. Look at what lengths you've attained, compare you to ultimately yourself, concentrate on you, on your results, and about how you have improved your outcomes. This will both inspire you and increase your self-esteem.

11. Spend additional time with supportive people (and less time with damaging people)

Even though you concentrate on being kind towards other folks (and yourself) and on replacing a perfectionism habit, it'll be hard to keep the self-esteem up if the most crucial influences in your daily life drag it down on a regular or regular basis. So make changes in the insight you get, choose to invest less time with folks who are anxious perfectionists, unkind or unsupportive of your dreams or goals and spend additional time with positive, uplifting individuals who have more human being and kinder requirements and means of considering things and consider what you read, pay attention to watching too. Spend less time with an internet discussion board, with reading a publication or viewing a TV-show if you feel it certainly makes you uncertain of yourself and if it certainly makes you think more adversely towards yourself.

Then spend enough time you used to invest in this information source on, for example, reading books, blogs, websites, and hearing podcasts that help you and that produce you are feeling good about yourself.

12. Keep in mind the whys of high self-esteem

What is a simple way to remain constant with doing something? As stated above: keep in mind the most crucial explanations why you do it. So remind yourself of the whys at the beginning of the article to do yourself a favor to remain motivated to focus on your self-esteem and also to make it an urgent priority.

Carrying this out and keeping these powerful reasons at heart has done amazing things for me. I am hoping it can do the same for you.

Chapter 11
10 Methods for Enhancing Your Self-Esteem

1. **Be nice to yourself**

That little voice that lets you know you're killing' it (or not), is a lot more powerful than you may think. Try to do yourself a favor and, if you undertake slip up, make an effort to solve any mental poison. A good guideline is to talk with yourself just as that you'd get hold of your mates. This is hard initially, but practice makes perfect. If you need a few tips, check out our techniques for speaking yourself up.

2. **You need to be you**

Comparing yourself to other folks ultimately, is a surefire way to begin feeling crummy. Make an effort to concentrate on your own goals and accomplishments, rather than to calculate them against someone else's. No one needs that kind of pressure.

3. Get moving

Exercise is a superb way to increase inspiration, practice environment goals, and build self-confidence. Breaking perspiration also cues your body to release endorphin, the feel-good hormones.

4. Nobody's perfect

Always make an effort to be the best version of yourself, but it's also important to accept that perfection can be an unrealistic goal.

5. Understand that everyone makes mistakes

You've surely got to make errors to find out and grow, so do not defeat yourself up, for instance, if you forget to press CTRL+S on the super-important task. Everyone's been there.

6. Concentrate on what you can transform

It's easy to get hung through to everything that is a way of your control, but it won't achieve much. Instead, make an effort to concentrate your energy on determining things that are inside your monitor and viewing your skill about them.

7. Do what makes you happy

If you spend some time doing the items you love, you're much more likely to believe positively. Make an effort to routine in just a little you-time every day. Whether that's time spent reading, cooking food, or simply conking from the couch for a little bit, if it certainly makes you happy, make time for this.

8. Celebrate the tiny stuff

You got through to time today! You poached your eggs to perfection! Celebrating small victories is a superb way to create confidence and begin feeling better about yourself.

9. Be considered a pal

Being helpful and considerate to other folks will undoubtedly enhance their feeling, but it'll also cause you to feel excellent about yourself

10. Encompass yourself with a supportive squad

Find people who cause you to feel great about yourself

and prevent those who tend to result in your negative thinking.